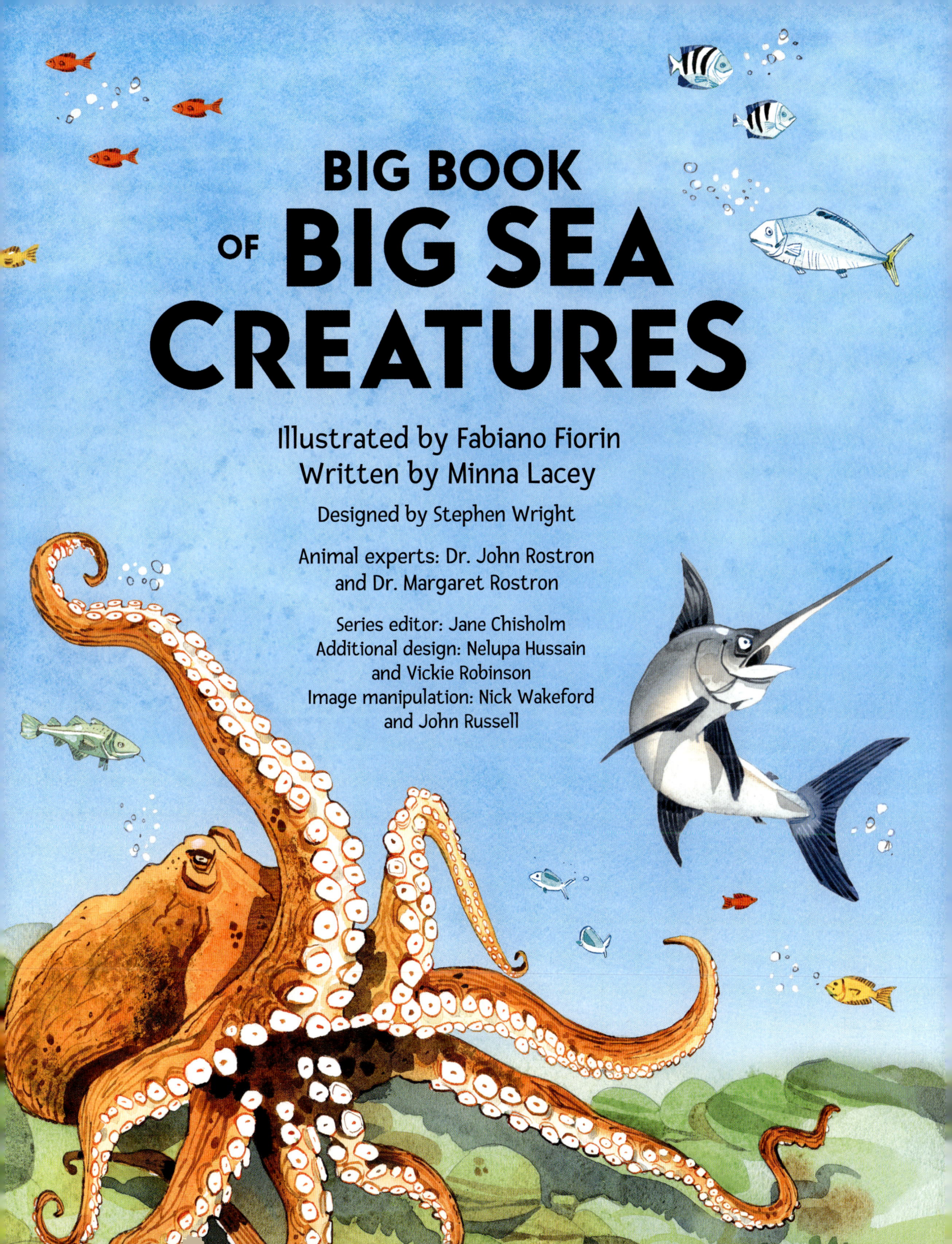

Coral reef

A coral reef is home to all sorts of amazing sea creatures. It is made from the skeletons of lots of tiny animals and takes thousands of years to grow.

Remora fish

White-tipped reef sharks are named after the white tips on their fins.

A **parrotfish** has teeth outside its jaws to help it crunch up coral to eat.

A **lionfish** has spiky fins with poisonous tips.

Octopuses, squid and jellyfish

Octopuses, squid and jellyfish have soft bodies and no shell. They have writhing arms or poisonous tentacles to help them catch prey.

A **common Atlantic octopus** has eight arms. It lies waiting in the rocks, then quickly grabs crabs or shrimp to eat.

A **lion's mane jellyfish** is the biggest jellyfish in the world. It floats near the surface and lives for only a year.

Each arm has powerful suckers to catch and hold onto prey.

Its tentacles are so long they could stretch across the length of a tennis court.

This octopus can change its shade to blend in with its background.

Killer whales have the largest dorsal fins of any whale or dolphin. Some fins grow 2m (6ft) high – as tall as a man.

A **humpback whale** is a powerful swimmer that often leaps out of the water.

Animals called barnacles grow on its skin.

Mammals

Some of the biggest and most extraordinary animals in the sea are vast mammals that swim and hunt underwater but come to the surface to breathe.

South American sea lions hunt for fish, squid and small penguins close to the shore.
Length: over 2½m (8ft)

Lift the pages to see ocean mammals drawn roughly to scale.

Atlantic walruses use their tusks for fighting and hauling themselves onto the Arctic ice.
Length: up to 3m (10ft)

Steller's sea lion males have a thick neck and hairy mane, like a lion.
Length: about 3m (10ft)

Killer whales are the largest kind of dolphin.
Length: up to 10m (33ft)

Fin whales are the second longest whale after the blue whale.
Length: up to 27m (89ft)

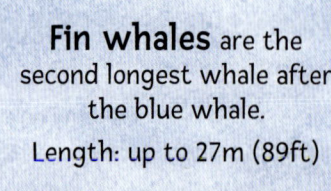

Inside its mouth are hundreds of plates that act as a net for catching tiny shrimp-like creatures called krill.

Blue whales are the biggest creatures that have ever lived. They make a loud rumbling noise that can be heard from far across the ocean.
Length: over 30m (100ft) – longer than two buses parked end to end.

Sperm whales are the biggest hunters in the ocean. They often attack giant squid deep below the surface.

Blue whales breathe through two blow holes on top of their head.

Southern elephant seals get their name from the male's big nose, which looks a bit like an elephant's trunk.
Length: up to 5m (16ft)

Bottlenose dolphins are highly intelligent and live in warm waters.
Length: 4m (13ft)

Leopard seals are fierce hunters that grab fish, small seals and penguins to eat.
Length: more than 3m (10ft)

Common long-beaked dolphins swim fast in groups, called pods, of up to a thousand dolphins.
Length: 2½m (8ft)

Dugongs graze on sea grass close to the shore. Unlike seals, they cannot live on land.
Length: up to 3m (10ft)

West Indian manatees move slowly near the surface, grazing on plants.
Length: 4m (13ft)

Humpback whale males sing a magical song that lasts for many hours.
Length: up to 16m (52ft)

Sperm whales dive deeper than any other mammal and can stay underwater for up to two hours.
Length: up to 18m (60ft)

Animals with shells

Many sea creatures have soft bodies with hard shells or bony skeletons on the outside, to give them protection from hungry predators.

All sea turtles have a shell on their backs – except the **leatherback sea turtle**, which has a tough, leathery skin instead.

A **giant clam** has a huge shell with four or five folds in it. It can live for 100 years and stays in the same place all its life.

This is the clam's mouth. It uses it to suck up tiny animals called plankton.

This bluish shade is produced by plants called algae that live on the clam.

The **emperor nautilus** has a striking brown-and-white shell with many compartments inside. It swims along by sucking in and shooting out jets of water.

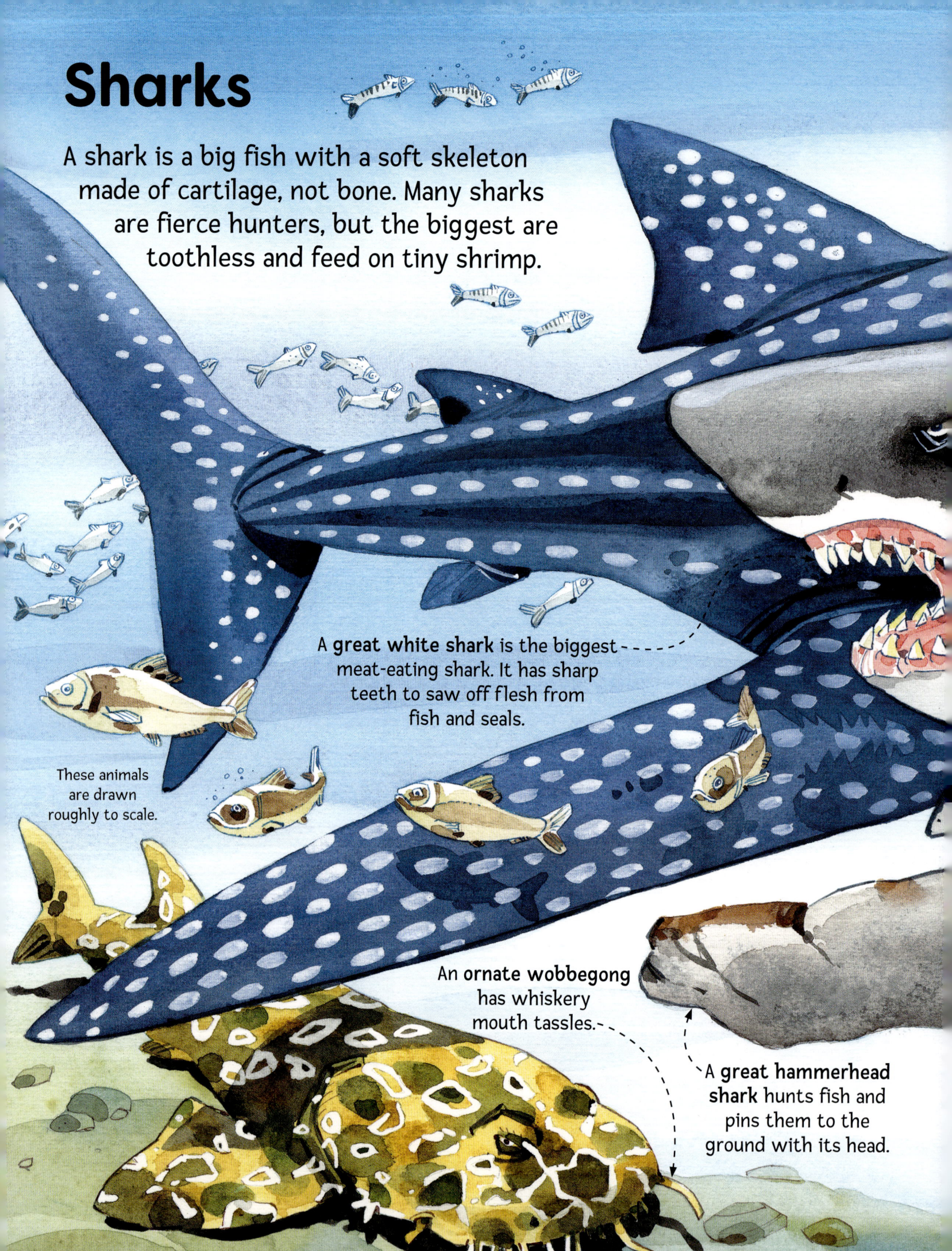

Sharks

A shark is a big fish with a soft skeleton made of cartilage, not bone. Many sharks are fierce hunters, but the biggest are toothless and feed on tiny shrimp.

A **great white shark** is the biggest meat-eating shark. It has sharp teeth to saw off flesh from fish and seals.

These animals are drawn roughly to scale.

An **ornate wobbegong** has whiskery mouth tassles.

A **great hammerhead shark** hunts fish and pins them to the ground with its head.

A **blue shark** has a slender body and is blue on top. It feeds on schools of fish and squid.

These **horse-eye jacks** are no bigger than rabbits.

A **goblin shark** is pink with a strange, beak-like snout. It lives in deep, dark waters.

Large front flippers help it move swiftly through the water. The turtle grows to a massive 3m (10ft) in length – that's as long as a tiger.

Atlantic lobsters are one of the largest lobsters. In real life, they're four times as long as this.

Its eyes move in different directions.

Its bigger claw is used for crushing crabs and fish to eat.

A **whale shark** is the biggest kind of fish. It has no teeth and grows to a massive 14m (46ft) – that's longer than a bus.

Sharks breathe through these gill slits.

A full-grown **epaulette shark** has a large black spot on its shoulder.

This **horse conch** is a large snail with a soft body and a hard shell to hide in. It hunts whelks and oysters.

A **horseshoe crab** lives on the sea floor. As it gets bigger, it sheds its old shell then starts growing a new one.

The **mantis shrimp** likes to hide in burrows in the sand. It stabs prey with its sharp claws.

Red hermit crabs live inside empty snail shells. As they grow, they look for bigger shells to move into.

Big fish

All fish breathe through gills at the sides of their heads. Most fish have a skeleton made of bone – except sharks and rays.

Mahi mahi have huge foreheads and long dorsal fins along their backs.
Length: up to 2m (6½ft)

Dorsal fin

Bluefin tuna are one of the fastest and biggest bony fish.
Length: up to 3m (10ft)

The gills are under here.

Humphead wrasse are some of the largest fish that live on coral reefs. They have a big bulge on their heads.
Length: up to 2m (6½ft)

Giant moray eels hide in rocky crevices during the day and hunt at night.
Length: up to 2½m (8ft)

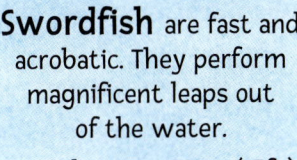

This sharp, sword-shaped bill is used to slash at prey.

Swordfish are fast and acrobatic. They perform magnificent leaps out of the water.
Length: up to 4½m (15ft)

Lift the pages to see big fish drawn roughly to scale.

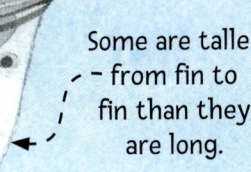

Some are taller from fin to fin than they are long.

Ocean sunfish are the largest kind of bony fish. They often swim slowly near the surface.
Length: up to 3½m (12ft)

An **ocean sunfish** gobbles up jellyfish. Its tough skin protects it from getting stung.

A **humphead wrasse** swishes its fins to move but keeps its tail still.

A **tiger shark** has dark stripes on its back. It feeds in shallow waters at night.

It can bite through the bodies of big sea turtles with its teeth.

Young **zebra sharks** have yellow and black stripes that disappear as they grow.

A **basking shark** is the world's second largest fish, after the whale shark. It grows to a length of 10m (33ft) – as long as two elephants.

It swims along with its enormous jaws open wide like a net to catch small shrimp and plants.

Biggest, fastest, longest...

The **southern elephant seal** is the BIGGEST of all seals, sea lions or walruses.

The **whale shark** is the BIGGEST FISH in the ocean. It gulps down water in its enormous mouth to catch very tiny animals and plants to eat.

The **sailfish** is one of the world's FASTEST fish. It can swim over 100km/h (62mph).

This **Japanese spider crab** has the biggest leg span of any crab: 4m (13ft) from claw to claw.

The world's biggest reptile is a **saltwater crocodile**. It weighs 1,000 kg (2,200lbs) – the same as a small car.

The **humpback anglerfish** lives in the DEEPEST part of the ocean. It hunts 2km (6,600ft) below the surface.

There is a light here to attract prey for the fish to gobble up.

Giant moray eels have sharp teeth for tearing the flesh of small fish, crabs or octopuses.

Conger eels are often found in shipwrecks and rocky pools. They feed on crabs, shrimp and octopuses.

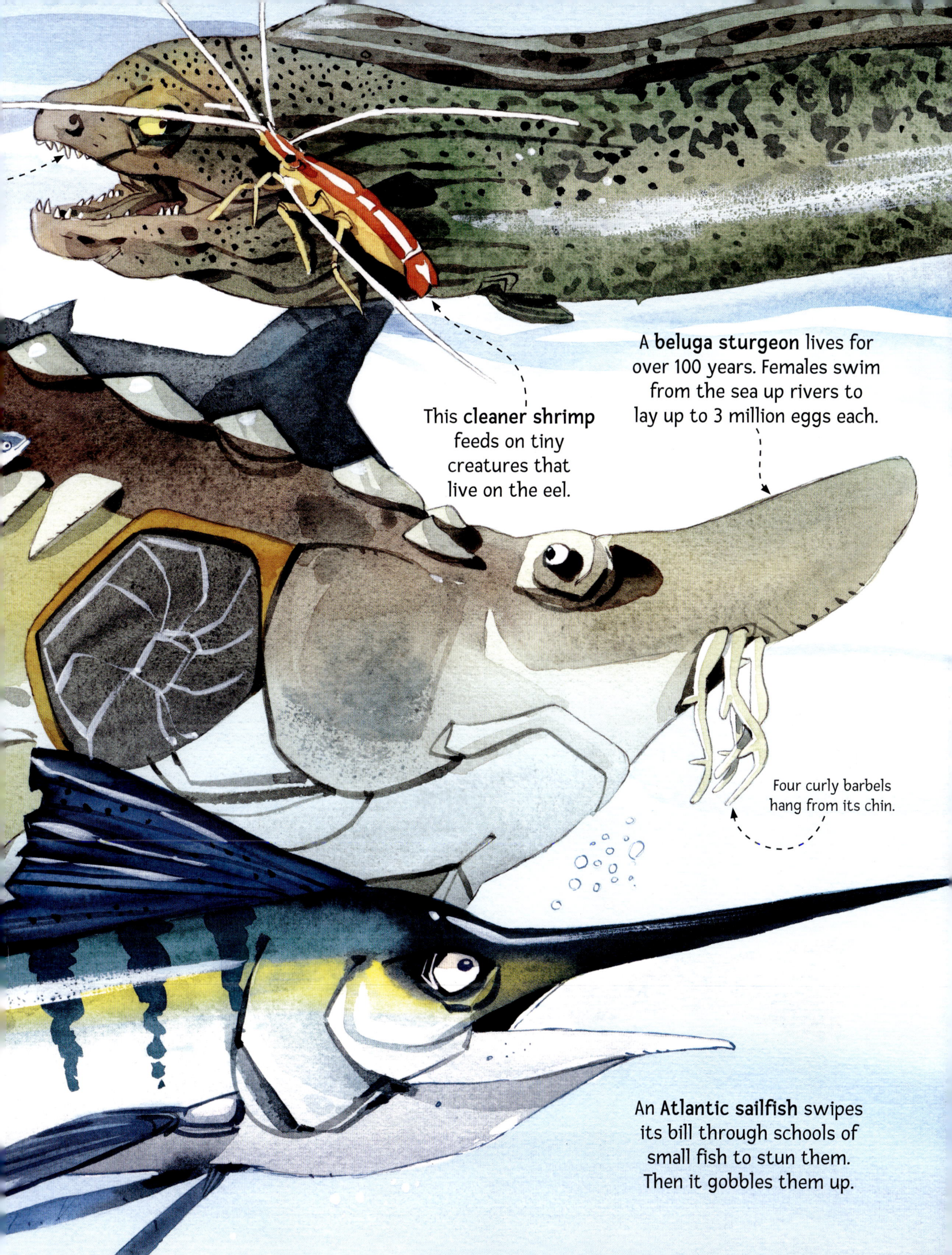

This **cleaner shrimp** feeds on tiny creatures that live on the eel.

A **beluga sturgeon** lives for over 100 years. Females swim from the sea up rivers to lay up to 3 million eggs each.

Four curly barbels hang from its chin.

An **Atlantic sailfish** swipes its bill through schools of small fish to stun them. Then it gobbles them up.

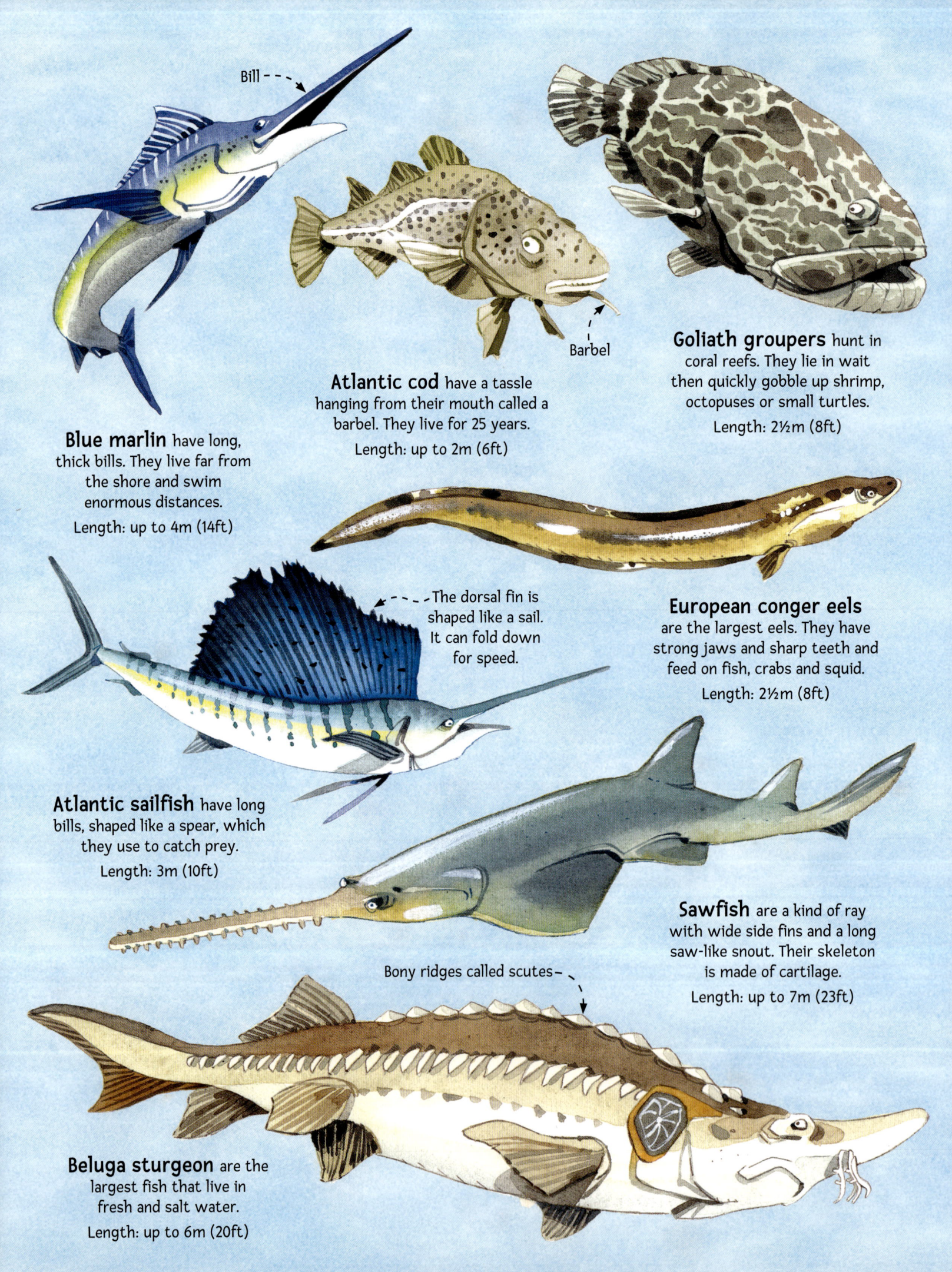

Usborne Quicklinks

For links to exciting websites about sea creatures with videos and activities, scan the QR code or go to **usborne.com/Quicklinks** and type in the keywords **sea creatures**.

Usborne Publishing is not responsible for the content of external websites. Children should be supervised online. Please follow the online safety guidelines at **usborne.com/Quicklinks**

This edition first published in 2025 by Usborne Publishing Limited, 83-85 Saffron Hill, London EC1N 8RT, United Kingdom. usborne.com Copyright © 2025, 2017, 2010 Usborne Publishing Limited. The name Usborne and the Balloon logo are registered trade marks of Usborne Publishing Limited. All rights reserved. No part of this publication may be reproduced or used in any manner for the purpose of training artificial intelligence technologies or systems (including for text or data mining), stored in retrieval systems or transmitted in any form or by any means without prior permission of the publisher. First published in America 2010. This edition first published 2025. UE.